LATOYA LAWRENCE

Wellness In Style

Thrive In Your Lifestyle

Contents

I

About The Author

LaToya Lawrence is a native of Queens, New York and is the author of four other previously published titles including **Harmonic Inspirations** *and* **God Has The Last Word**

One

Welcome

You are welcome to join as I share small parts of my life as examples of the diversity that is within us individuals while encouraging and inspiring healthy lifestyle and well-being suitable to one's own preferred way of living.

Our mind and spirit need to be fed just as well as our bodies.

Harmonic alignment in personal environment promotes physical comfort, mental stimulation, and a spiritual peace which creates balance.

It is not about what is so-called normal as much as it is about what is healthy when going about individual wellness and how a person obtains fulfillment.

If we do not pick out and wear the correct fit within

accordance to our own specific foot size in proportion to area to breathe, we just make the walk unnecessarily hard to bear.

Two

Calmness

When I think of calm I think of silence, tranquility, serenity.

A state of undisturbed peace—a soothing pacifying gentleness displayed within oneself and within others who are self-possessed in their coolness of composure—even in the most difficult of times.

Sometimes there is nothing better than the sound of still quietness within the walls of a room.

Our body laid down comfortably, eyes closed, mind at peace—a pleasant vibration of relaxation.

No noise, no irritation, no intrusion.

We all need quiet time. Time to be alone, time for us, and time for ourselves to ruminate, deliberate, meditate, and alleviate.

I have a calm nature.

I am a loner, the type who does not care to be bothered most of the time, yet I am a laid back, easy-going, and out-going person who can naturally be a people person when it comes to the right type of people who I relate to.

There are times when we must make allowances for those who we differ from who are incongruent to, or incompatible with.

We are not always going to come into agreement or get along with everyone. We are also not going to be fond of everyone who we cross paths with or encounter either and that is perfectly fine just if we try as best, we can avoid conflict.

When conflict cannot be avoided due to whatever circumstance because sometimes confrontations are necessary depending on the situation for things that arise or that need to be resolved or brought out into the open there should be a non-violent way in conducting one's behavior while tempers may get heated and uncontrolled.

* * *

Where True Peace Of Mind Comes From

Peace of mind is priceless. One of the precious gems that is bestowed by spirit.

Gained anywhere else is not true peace. Only a temporary state of comfort relied upon by whatever is satisfying for those limited periods of time.

Invaluable within value as when comfort wears out—or no longer exists—out goes the conditional description of what was providing one's peace.

Now the true inner peace derived through spirit that cannot be deciphered through veiled eyes and which remains undisturbed when chaotic events strike is not dependent upon tangible items, favorable circumstances, or material things.

This peace is solely dependent upon what is impalpable. What is out of grasp and maintained by the unreachable.

What we see touch and feel will not last, but what is beyond the sense of what appears is forever lasting, bringing great peace and protection beyond what we can feel, touch, or see.

So just be and let the spirit set one free.

Three

Anxiety

Anxiety was never a part of my life or something I ever had to battle with though I can relate to things in life that may cause strain.

I am aware there are a lot of people who are anxious and apprehensive. Some are prone to anxiety attacks.

Life, of course, can be stressful for many, but the stresses of life do not have to stress us out or get us down.

It is all about where our priorities lie and what we place emphasis on.

We must be on top of things and not on the bottom.

Know, realize, and accept that certain things are just out of our control.

And why do we want to be in control of things that are not meant for us to control unless we are granted a way to attain and utilize that control?

Worry, apprehension, doubt, and fear are not going to get us anywhere.

All those feelings do is cause an addition to the degree of negative emotion that further initiates tension, agitation, and misgiving.

Do not torture oneself. Anxiety itself is not the culprit or enemy.

We all naturally have reasonable worries or concerns due to predicaments or conditions that are foreboding and that threatens one's equanimity.

Though, some people do worry unnecessarily about things that are not worth worrying about.

They place great worth and value on keeping up with the latest trends, and social standing in society.

What matters, interests, or disturbs a lot of people can absolutely have no type of affect or impact on certain others as there is a variety of diversity within our ever-changing world.

However, what remains unchanging is that God is forever in control of all things.

* * *

Stress On The Job

A lot of us would love to have our dream job. The careers of our choice to accomplish and excel in.

There are some who are fortunate and who get lucky enough to acquire an occupation suitable to their desires without too much hassle or in a quick time frame.

For many others, we may get jobs we like to support our financial needs for the time being until we find or attain the occupation in life that we prefer to do or achieve.

Some of us will take on jobs and work in places where we truly do not want to be on account of circumstances related to job applications being turned down, a too far out location to travel to, and so on.

Some of us may be overqualified for certain jobs or underqualified.

Nevertheless, we do what we must do to survive and make an honest living when the time is right for us to go out into the world.

People should go and get a job when they are ready and not because they feel pressured by judgmental people who have not walked in their shoes or who do not know their life story, or what is going on in their life and the individual's life design.

Everyone who does not work is not lazy, a bum, or worthless.

It is the one who never plans or desires to ever make a living for themselves who are the losers.

Some people do not care what type of job they have or where they work at as long as they get a paycheck.

To each his or her own.

I have worked jobs I did not like, and I have worked jobs that I enjoyed, yet I would eventually get tired because they were not my passion.

Although I was good at the jobs that I did they were not where I really wanted to be. Writing was always where my heart was—something I was born and always meant to do.

However, when I was in certain working environments my job was more like fun to me and came easily even if the work I did was challenging.

So, when others would complain of their job being stressful (and we were in the same establishment) I did not understand why. If anything, the job was therapeutic in that it helped to occupy time in a constructive beneficial way while exercising physical and mental stamina.

We are all unique individuals with various mentalities—and who knows what may have been going on in the personal lives of those who contributed to their own stress on the job as some people stress themselves out.

Some are just not delighted by the same work that others take pleasure in.

Then, there are the problems that are brought on by coworkers, managers or customers/clients if one works in fields that cater to interaction with consumers.

* * *

Stress In The Home

Anxiety comes in different forms and is caused by several factors according to why the instance occurs.

Some people have anxiety disorders.

The stress of marital or romantic relationships, parenting, or other issues can interrupt a person's thought-process and behavioral patterns.

People need effective ways of dealing with anxiety caused stress and there is no one fix for all people.

It is important to recognize exactly what it is causing one's anxiety and if there is any merit to the energy.

The best remedy for anxiety and stress is spirituality.

Rely on the divine to carry the burden of our pressures and strains.

When doubts filled my mind, your comfort gave me renewed hope and cheer.- Psalms 94: 19

Give your burdens to the LORD, and he will take care of you. He will not permit the godly to slip and fall.- Psalms 55: 22

* * *

Instrumental Advice

Music is one of the best pleasures on earth!

What would we do without songs, lyrics, and instrumental tunes that soothe, heal, and make us happy?

Music enlivens and revives us.

Music can make us forget about the annoyance that was torturing our minds or taunting our emotions.

Music is an escape that can take us away into inspiration and rejuvenation.

Turn on the music and turn that stress or anxiety into a dance fest.

Four

Energy

Energy is the force of life. Everything is made up of energy, and everything is run by energy.

Whether it is by electromagnetic waves/radiation in which manifests as a capacity to provide activation in physical or chemical resources through process, or from the power derived from the utilization of our physical and mental abilities and what we exert.

If one is born with extra sensory perception, endowed with heightened awareness, they may constantly be bombarded with all types of energy vibration exuded from others in addition to the inner and outer realm of things.

We can tap into ethereal dimensions through preternatural capacity as we are naturally connected to the spirit world while we continue to have our human experience here on this physical plane.

There is a great difference between average people and people who are highly sensitive spiritually.

There are also some who may fit somewhere in between, and so on as individuals can be made up of a combination of variations when it comes to inborn traits or tendencies.

Though those of us born with extra sensory perception are predisposed to feel and perceive things beyond the range of what is considered normal—we all have a propensity to react to energy or the lack thereof.

* * *

Energy is that robust vitality to moves us into action.

Positiveness makes us feel good if one is an individual who responds to good stimulation because there are people out there who feed and who thrive off negative energy—it is in their nature to do so and it is within their state of alignment.

Some people love to be bad and enjoy unpleasant/distasteful attitudes or unscrupulous behavior—it keeps them alive while negativity is their form of positivity.

Whereas negative energy may or would dull the spirits of decent or healthy-minded people, negative-minded people are enlivened and motivated by what is not welcome.

* * *

To me it has never been about what is so-called "normal" (whatever that is supposed to be), or about what is accustomed to by many.

It has always been about what is healthy and in harmony with one.

And for me, positive energy does it for me every time!

Energy is more powerful and impactful than some give it credit for regarding the spiritual aspect that can affect both the mental and emotional well-being.

Physical energy helps to keep us moving at a steady pace.

The physical, mental, spiritual and emotional all contribute to mood, method and mobility.

Though one is not always contingent upon the other as we are all unique individuals who can cope, persevere, and be content regardless of circumstances.

Nevertheless, when we are fully functioning to a satisfying degree within all we may feel and do our best.

* * *

I am a bubbly person. I have been high-spirited since my youth.

Many lively, animated people are so charismatic because they have an essence and effervescence that tends to radiate inspiration in others as they uplift and bring comfort with their sanguine air that becomes contagious in their light-hearted carefree attitudes.

Energy is about letting go to experience the flow of verve.

Energy is a punch that never knocks us out. A blow packed to spark drive, bounce, zeal, strength and exuberance.

If one is of a positive nature, then it is important and beneficial to associate and occupy themselves with others who demonstrate positiveness in themselves and in their life.

Authenticity is rare, but whenever it is fiercely displayed by ones who exhibit their realness in everyday life—they are totally phenomenal!

Us good-natured individuals should endeavor to bring out the best in one another as we can serve as compliments to each other while manifesting positive energy into the universe through goodwill.

Five

Food And Beverage

It matters what we put into our bodies.

We should love and respect ourselves. I know I always have.

Food and drink provide us with the energy and necessary nutrients that our bodies need to perform correctly if we eat right.

Although, of course, there are numerous factors as to why everyone cannot maintain proper health on certain diets—even ones catered to good health—due to special diets or dietary restrictions.

We do benefit greatly from consuming lots of fruits, vegetables, beans, legumes and seeds.

Nature comes with the best remedies to aid us to better living. Clean eating in the purest of possible forms. The best diets are vegan, vegetarian or polo pescatarian.

I have been a vegan/vegetarian for about 35 years.

The vegan diet consists of eating absolutely nothing derived from animal sources. The polo pescatarian diet is a type of vegetarian that eats poultry and seafood but no red meat or pork.

Realistically everyone is not going to turn vegetarian, nor does everyone desire to and that is perfectly fine, if anyone is health conscious, they should heed to monitor their intakes of unhealthy fats, oils, sugars, fried foods and so on.

All foods marketed for vegans are not suitable for their health, that is why instead of buying processed foods we are better off preparing our own.

* * *

Take Care Of That Heart

It is so important to take care of the heart and to keep those arteries as clean as possible.

Some people are genetically predisposed to have coronary events and one never knows when a heart attack or stroke may strike.

It does not matter what age we are it all depends on how we treat and care for our bodies by eating the proper foods, doing suitable exercise, getting significant rest, refraining from toxic substances which in the short term or long run cause harm or premature death, and avoiding unnecessary situations that can or will cause stress.

Go to the doctor for regular check-ups. Always inquire them to further investigate anything that seems abnormal/out of range where health professionals may overlook or not pick up right away or at all.

Get second opinions on things too if need be.

We cannot afford to let the beats of our lives conk out on us. We must keep that clock ticking for as long as the beat goes on!

* * *

Coffee/Coffee Addiction/Caffeine

Just to clarify: There are people who drink their coffee every morning or maybe three or four times a week and there is absolutely nothing out of the ordinary or wrong with that.

On the other hand, there are those who rely on numerous cups of coffee at a continuous pace or rate and use the beverage as a crutch.

A lot of people are hooked on coffee.

Whereas some people like and drink different varieties of coffee for the taste, some claim they need the beverage to help wake them up in the morning, and some claim they need the beverage to help keep them up during the late hours of the night.

Tea also contains a significant amount of caffeine which will keep one alert and up all night if they drink enough of it.

Tea is a lighter and healthier beverage to consume in comparison to coffee as there are numerous herbal teas loaded with an array of medicinal properties and nutritional benefits, yet they naturally do not contain any caffeine like regular black tea does, and that is a good thing.

Nevertheless, many are not able to function without their cups of coffee and I have wondered if the instance is psychological as well as part addiction for a lot of people.

I have never been a constant or heavy coffee drinker.

I would drink a large French vanilla cappuccino occasionally, but after the one cup, I was not able to drink anymore of the beverage within the same day of each other.

My appetite and body would not allow me to ingest an excess of coffee as it would give me a stomachache. There was a definite limit as to how much I was able to drink before it could wreak havoc in my constitution.

The one cup of cappuccino on occasion was enough to satisfy my fancy, anyhow.

Coffee was never a beverage for me to get hooked on. I am a juice, water, and soy-milk junkie.

It has been years since I have drank coffee, in fact, it has been a decade, and I do not at all miss the taste of it.

I stay away from any source of caffeine as much as possible.

All my coffees used to be decaffeinated I barely drink black iced tea for this reason. I do not even want a little bit of it in my system but just as long as it's not a part of my daily intake and everyday lifestyle.

I have done a lot of twelve-hour day and night shifts as well as overnight shifts through my work schedules in the past and I have never depended on or needed any type of "pick me up" stimulant or substance to focus with or keep me going.

I have never even considered such a thing as an option. I radiate my own stamina and energy through healthy well-being and determination.

Some people really let that coffee get the best of them. The coffee has them going crazy. Some go into fits if they cannot get their dose of coffee.

I know, I've seen it first-hand with quite a few susceptible individuals.

These people must have their coffee five and six times a day, maybe even more, depending on how their day is going, if they run out of coffee, and if they can afford to buy more at the given time.

Some of these people drink coffee like a fish in water or like it may be going out of style.

Six

Supplements

I have been a vitamin junkie for years.

During my teens I used to frequent health food stores and vitamin shops while I was on the path to being a strict vegan at the time.

From my personal experience vitamin supplements really do work. They are very beneficial for the body and overall wellness.

All supplements are not created equally so when making a purchase be sure to research the company who manufactures the vitamins and always read the ingredient labels on bottled supplements before deciding whether the product is suitable.

Call up the company customer service line if desired to inquire whatever information about the item that may not be revealed on the content label.

I was one to always investigate what I put into my body aware of the fact that some companies are not always honest about their ethical practices.

They will lie and tell us anything to profit financially—but this is nothing out of the ordinary, it happens in all areas of life and business.

There are trusted brands of herbal and vitamin supplements that I have stuck with for years completely satisfied with the results and with the maintenance that have contributed to my good health.

Regardless of how well supplements can work we are to not overdo it.

Sometimes some of us can get carried away and depending on our constitution we do not want to harm our kidneys or liver because too much of anything can have side effects.

So have fun on the journey to sustain a lifestyle of vitality but take it easy!

I highly recommend supplements that are vegan/vegetarian suitable, non GMO, without fillers, and that are labeled with legitimate seals and certifications of high quality, assuring the product consists of laboratory testing to confirm accuracy of contents as well as safety of consumption.

Seven

Ailments

No one is perfect and neither are our bodies.

Some people have physical or mental ailments that may reduce the quality of their lives and get them down.

No one wants to continuously be in pain. No one wants to live life suffering.

As one who has worked in health care settings, I have seen all kinds of illnesses and afflictions—not to mention firsthand experience I already had before I ever entered the Healthcare field.

People have different ways of handling and coping with their conditions and situations. Some people become bitter and take their anger and frustration out on others. Some accept their predicaments to become blessings to others in ways they never imagined.

They inspire and encourage others to overcome their disorders or disabilities by not allowing limitations or labels to be placed upon them.

Some ailments are minor while others are severe and bring challenges into one's life.

We grow to become stronger and more durable throughout the struggles of life, but no challenge is bigger than the human spirit and no challenge is too big for God.

* * *

A Common Ailment Many Of Us Have: Osteoarthritis

Throughout life many of us have put a lot of wear and tear on our bodies.

I have been very active doing plenty of heavy lifting and bending in my personal and professional activities.

Strenuous movements if done with the proper body mechanics at the correct pace also exercise the muscles, however, performing tasks which over exert the body to cause unnecessary strain and pressure may be harmful if or when not proceeding with caution.

Accidents and injuries are often the results of minor or major aches and pains, depending on the extent of the predicament.

With most of us a little wear and tear is natural over time, and we may develop osteoarthritis.

It also helps to eat and intake nutritious anti-inflammatory foods, herbs, and vitamin supplements as they are very beneficial in the restoration and maintenance of specific bodily tissues and functions.

Physical therapy is also helpful, though, an appointment every once a week to get a massage and penetrating rub down is not effective at all, not in my opinion, as the procedure did absolutely nothing for me in relieving my discomfort.

One would need a therapeutic treatment everyday consecutively to heal and improve dramatically. Not to mention the cost of such clinical visits if one is not covered by medical insurance or must pay out of pocket.

I refused to waste my time and medical coverage on sessions that were not serving any purpose.

We can purchase our own massaging and therapeutic gadgets and equipment to aid within the process of bodily repair and pamper.

For extreme symptoms of a condition, one should, of course, remain under the close supervision of a medical professional in case there is need for pain medication and/or further radiology testing.

Wellness In Style

Eight

Disease And Spiritual Healing

Some diseases are fatal, some diseases are life altering, some diseases are just an annoyance and some diseases are temporary and curable.

No disease or ailment defines or determines one's identity or position in life.

I had my very first mammogram during the year 2019. My primary care physician had suggested for me to get one prior when I first entered my forties as a routine precaution.

I do not know of anyone in my family to have ever had breast cancer and aside from there being no history of it in the lives of my relatives, I never had any personal concern regarding the issue.

I know bloodline is not a definite factor and that anyone can be at risk for breast cancer when it may not always be known or explained, nevertheless, I did not consider breast cancer a threat to me.

My test results came back normal as I had expected.

I know the thought of going through biopsies, treatments, having a mastectomy, or the possibility of an impending death is a grave matter for a lot of women and one that could be stressful and exhausting.

Yet, still and all, if I was diagnosed with the disease, I would handle the situation in an entirely different fashion.

When it was suspected I had a malignant growth on one of my ovaries during my teenage years up into early adulthood I was not fazed by the instance. I had already sensed and knew I had a mass before the doctors came to know and before I went through all the radiology testing and procedures I had undergone.

My mother at one point in her life had ovarian cancer and was lucky enough to defeat and survive it so I had a good idea of what was going on within my body with the pain and discomfort. I was not afraid or mentally or emotionally troubled by the experience at all.

I did not care, and I am still here.

As one very spiritual and very spiritually inclined it was revealed that I was never meant to fall fatally ill and die from any disease, it just was not in my destiny.

The power of healing is a very legitimate condition as I know my spirit, body, and mind is much stronger than an attack or threat of any foul disease.

I have already been put to the test.

The mass had mysteriously dissolved or disappeared when I was twenty-three without ever returning and I had never had any issues with my ovaries afterwards.

We have to leave everything in God's hands while using discernment to know what is ahead and how to take action. God is the one in control of all outcomes.

Nine

Suicide

People kill themselves for various reasons.

One never knows what is going on within another person's mind or what they are going through. I never looked at people who commit suicide as being cowards. If anything, it is the opposite.

I am in no way condoning the act, but it takes a lot of strength and courage to put an end to one's life.

Once the act is committed there is no turning back from it and the ones who embark on that journey dive into the unknown not knowing exactly where they are headed or what to expect.

I do not like it when or agree with people who declare that all people who kill themselves are headed straight to hell.

Only God knows where their souls/spirits will reside or rest. No one has the right to determine the destiny of everyone who commits suicide. God knows all of us inside out. He is a loving and compassionate God, and it is him alone who decides all our outcomes no matter what we do.

I cannot speak for everybody within the world but if many were honest a lot of people would admit that they wished they were never born.

They have desired one time or another to kill themselves or have even tried.

When I was in my teens and early adulthood people much older than me told me they had tried or wanted to. Fear of going to hell is what prevented some from doing it.

A lot of people want to die and leave this earth.

It is not because all these people cannot handle life or their circumstances. Some people are just tired. This world is a very sick place. A lot of terrible things are going on.

It costs too much to eat, pay rent, buy necessities. Society is overpopulated. There is excess violence, and so on.

There are beautiful and wonderful things to this life here on earth too, but I understand and can relate to how certain people feel.

Like I said before, I cannot speak for everyone, but I do not believe that many who contemplate or who have contemplated suicide want to cease from life itself.

I think they want to escape whatever unsavory, unfortunate, or undesirable reality they may be experiencing here on this earth. What they are probably hoping for is a blissful life apart from this world on what they project is on the other side of this place.

There are probably some who do want to cease life altogether too based on their perceptions or misconceptions of God and the nature of circumstance.

Suicide is a permanent solution to temporary predicaments. Situations, conditions, and circumstances can change but killing oneself cannot be unchanged once the act is committed.

We are all going to die one day there is no need to rush the process.

People who take their own lives bring heartache and pain to those who love them dearly. Their enemies or people who dislike them may be glad to see them go but not those who care about them.

No matter what one is going through suicide is not the path to head down. I would not want to be anywhere near that road it seems like a dark place to end up at.

Nevertheless, I do not criticize anyone who has felt or dealt with those feelings because I can look deeper into the route of things and grasp understanding.

Ten

Depression

Everyone gets depressed occasionally, it is perfectly normal.

It is okay to not be okay sometimes. We all deal with personal or life-related issues from time to time.

The temporary state of gloom or despondency is usually caused by some form of sadness or discontentment over situations or events that eventually come to pass.

A lingering depression that lasts longer than it should depending on the reason for why as there are exceptions such as in the case of losing loved ones through death, living in poverty, suffering long term illness and other grave occurrences that may take place giving rise to dejection or discouragement.

If depression becomes a problem to a point where it is interfering with one moving forward or handling the responsibilities in their life, then they should seek help or counsel from a trusted relative or friend.

Sometimes it is better to talk to people who know you and that you are well acquainted with compared to a stranger who may generalize, have preconceived notions, or jump to conclusions as some professionals will or often do.

If guidance from family or friends is not possible or unsuccessful, and circumstances are unable to be resolved then one may have to resort to and seek professional help from a therapist, counselor, or psychiatrist.

Also, if one is spiritual, they can always go to God.

If one is not spiritual and if one is open to it use the opportunity to get close to God and form a relationship with him to experience divine intervention and healing.

Eleven

Self-Care

A lot of us are sleep deprived due to our hectic schedules and demanding occupations in which can be time consuming.

The intent and determination to support ourselves, to maintain our lifestyles, and to conduct our business, often makes us less preoccupied in getting the proper rest.

We are more concerned with our personal and financial responsibilities.

Usually, our main priorities are to keep a roof over our heads, to keep enough food on the table, and to adequately pay our bills.

A good night's rest we desire and need at more times than certain others, yet put that behind, as we acquire to get the most important things done and out of the way before we attend to our own personal comforts.

I never let any of my obligations and goals deter me from properly taking care of myself, though.

Despite how many hours I put in and how often I must work to meet my needs and wants, I always make sure that I eventually eat a good meal, and that I am not overly exhausted.

We must do what we have to do to make an honest living and to survive, however, at the same time, we are not to run ourselves down within the process.

As I am a very spiritually inclined individual I give a lot of things to faith, without fret or worry, knowing and believing everything will carry out within alignment to what is required and to what is the most vital.

So, take out quality time to spend with loved ones and take out the necessary time to care for self and to enjoy the personal rewards of all the hard work and dedication.

* * *

Sometimes sleepy during the day?

The feeling of sleep will creep upon us when we do not get enough rest throughout the night.

Rest is pampering and healing as we are snugged comfortably in bed. Our bodies rejuvenate and our minds invigorate while we are asleep.

A good night's rest is satisfyingly expressed in a full whole-hearted stretch.

Twelve

Love Oneself

Do Not Allow Anyone To Steal The Joy That Resides Inside

* * *

It all starts within the home.

I had and was given so much love and attention at home that I never sorted out to find love elsewhere.

Love made me confident; love made me strong; love made me secure, and no one can take away what was instilled in me from the beginning.

I have very high self-esteem and I am very sure of myself I have never desired, needed, or looked for social acceptance or validation from anyone.

I do not understand people who do.

I do not like people who reflect their own insecurities and negativities onto me, and onto others who exude a genuine and a positive self-image, and attitude.

Those whose self-esteem is so low that they interpret self-assurance and strong sense of self as being full of oneself is all too self-telling.

It seems that some who are unable to reach a secure level of self-worth and self-value within themselves are more apt or prone to devalue the value others have for themselves.

Insecure individuals who have self-doubt, have doubt within others, only because they do not believe the possibilities in others, that are impossible for them.

Thirteen

Work

I don't like it when employers/managers try to take advantage of you because they know you are a good worker.

It has happened to me a few times.

I had a company I worked for have me fill in for another employee who was supposed to return to her schedule on day two of me covering her shift, yet she was able to call out again, and I got left hanging for two extra days on the job.

I ended up working four extra days straight or else I would have gotten penalized due to the fact management had no one else to cover for them.

If it was me who had called out like that it would not have been acceptable.

When I tried to get out of it one of the managers told me "No". And her excuse was "We can't get another associate like you and one as good as you for the particular assignment".

So, it was all about making the company look good never mind what I may have had planned on my days off.

I had just finished my own complete weekly schedule immediately prior to getting a call from a manager to fill in for what they claimed would be a two day fill in shift. I accepted to make extra money not to be conveniently "sentenced" to an assignment on account of another employee's irresponsibility.

I eventually walked out on them I had too much self-respect.

I understand when someone can be depended upon and/or does outstanding or exceptional work supervisors tend to heavily rely on them to come through and consider them to be a great representation of their establishment.

However, attempting to use someone who is an asset for one's own recognition and advancement within the workplace at the cost of depriving the employee of their own fair treatment is highly unethical.

After all, it is the employee doing and putting in all the work. Why not show appreciation by promoting them instead of keeping them in the same position only to benefit from them or because the managers fear their employee will eventually snatch up their job.

I have been on jobs where the supervisors did not even know what they were doing, they did not have a clue about how to properly do their job or how to manage the establishment, and they had to count on other employees who were under them to show and teach them the certain procedures in which they should have already had experience within, and known, in order to have obtained the positions they were in to begin with.

Many supervisors have not earned their way up honestly they were given their jobs either out of favoritism, because they may have had a relative pull some strings for them, or they just knew someone just as corrupt as they were who also abusively used their position to rise without deserving any of their working status.

I have had to phone up the corporate office on more than one of my employees at two of my workplaces within the past, and surely, the supervisors were investigated, and action was taken because I was in the right.

Things do not always play out so well when contacting head-quarters, of course, because there is also plenty of corruption within the corporate offices too.

* * *

Non Working People

To me, having a job does not make a person who they are.

There are employed people who are not about anything and who are not worth anything, they may have just gotten lucky, or were more fortunate in life than certain others.

Then, there are the unemployed who happen to be the most valuable and reasonable people on the planet.

There are many reasons some people do not have jobs or do not want to work.

Their grounds are not always on listless, baseless, or negative terms either and they do not owe anyone any explanations whatsoever.

Unless others have walked in these people's shoes they should not be so quick to stomp all over them.

Some people do not like to constantly be around other people. Some people may see the world in a different light than average or what is usual.

Some people want to be their own boss. Some people want to utilize their own talents in their own ways.

Some people have things going on around them in which may call for them to sort out before they make their significant turn unto their journey.

Some people are dealing with illnesses. One never knows what is going on in another person's life.

I am not saying this is the case for everyone, of course, there are unmotivated low-life bums who exist only to steal or to mooch off other decent people.

There are also those who are unable to hold a job and those who are too incompetent to work due to a lack of skills and a lack of proficiency, however, I am not talking about individuals within this category.

I am talking about good or okay people who just may have had a case of bad luck, a hard or difficult life, a spiritual dilemma, a celestial arrangement, or they just may have an unconventional outlook where they view things inexplicably but they are not bad or lazy people and they will get whatever they need to get together when the time is right for them.

The universe has a way of design, and a way of working things out.

* * *

To Sum It Up: A Job Does Not Define A Person's Worth

I was told twice one day by a mature (ninety-five year old) woman of experience that because of the way I look physically, and the way that I carry myself, I should be in movies.

This is not the first time I have been told these words and similar ones alike.

As a teen and young adult, some people would ask me if I was a model and would tell me that I could be one.

Another person told me they saw me as a movie actress type who was supposed to be writing screenplays.

Aside from other things, I could have been a lawyer or a psychologist if I had really wanted and chose to. I have both the smarts and the mindset.

The fact is, I never wanted a life in Hollywood to be broadcast on television, or to be photographed for magazines walking down the runway.

I never had the desire to be a legal representative or mental health specialist either.

Though many of us are qualified or can do or become professionals in more than one area, it does not mean this is a preferred career or path to seek. Jobs and job labels do not define us as individuals.

Even though there are narrow-minded misinformed people who believe the higher the title or higher the income, the higher the stature.

Someone who does not have a job or who has a job that is considered low rank in comparison to high-level/high-profile jobs can have far more integrity, intelligence, ability than the one touting their so-called credentials.

They may have just not gotten the right opportunity, could have fallen into hard times like I have mentioned before, did not believe enough within themselves or did not have any support.

There are several reasons and factors for why those who could achieve great heights do not.

A lot of people who are in positions of power or who hold positions that are praised within society are not as adequate as they think they are or would like to believe.

Many of them are nothing but shit!

They are as common as they come—there is nothing special about their existence.

Novel within character and mindset unlike the ordinary are what define true standing within its authenticity.

Fourteen

Sweet Soothing Memories

A lot of us have reflections of the past—savored memories—that bring nostalgia.

Remembrance of this kind is delightful to the senses and is beneficial through natural tendencies to incite happiness, sentiment, and endearment for a time that once was in our lives.

Looking back at old photos to reminisce is another pleasant reflective activity to recount precious forgotten or unforgotten events or occurrences that transpired.

Our minds are a place where we store and collect. Where we deliberate and rationalize. It is also a place where impressions materialize. Reminders of events depicted within visionary, auditory or conceptual representation.

Our reflection of memories. Indelibly painted imprints and images embedded in the brain.

Somethings are forgotten. Some things are remembered as clearly as day. Sometimes what was totally forgotten can be triggered by something to be recalled again in an instant.

Some memories of things or events become cloudy or totally forgotten to never emerge from the fog of forgetfulness.

Memories that reflect to us are a great benefit bestowed to us upon nature. A blessing to our well-being.

Good, bad, and neutral memories serve to assist within our review, study, attest, and mirror of what we experience and consciously, unconsciously, or subconsciously absorb.

* * *

Pieces Of My Childhood

I am a proud child of the 70's.

We had some fun and fabulous toys made of excellent quality back then. I had a lot of items to play with, too many to name.

To mention a few that I loved and enjoyed was The Fisher Price Movie Viewer. I only had the Snow White, Sesame Street (Cookie Monster in the kitchen), and Mickey Mouse (Lonesome

Ghosts) cartridges. This particular tool was great because we could view the animated films forward and backward, either fast or slow.

The Tree Tots by Kenner were one of my very favorites. I had the Treehouse, the Lighthouse, and the Amusement Park!

The little Tots and their dog were awesome!

I constantly sniffed my adorable Strawberry Shortcake and Lemon Meringue dolls as they were sweetly scented with fragrance. I had the adorable Snail that would move on its own as it rode Strawberry Shortcake and her friend in the attached carriage.

Dancerella was a ballerina that stood on her toes and actually spun around in poses. I played with her a lot.

When I was growing up, we were not like the kids today who play with a new toy for a short time, get tired of it, then want a different new toy to play with.

No matter what additional toy was added to our collection, we played with the old and new ones all year around for years until we completely wore them out—I know I did.

I still had some of my old toys into my adulthood stored away before I moved from my childhood home.

We will never have toys and other objects such as the ones that we had back in the day when everything was so exciting.

I am sure the generation before me feels the same way about the era they were born and grew up in.

***

The home decor style of the 60's and 70's were not just for hippies and gypsy fortune tellers.

Whether one called them door beads or beaded curtains—bead adornments that decorated the entrances of doorway rooms in the home and within establishments offered a cozy and enchanting ambience to settings that a lot of individuals could appreciate.

I remember as a young child during the late seventies and early eighties, walking through the clear-colored beads that hung from my home, clasping them open, loving the sounds they made while they hit up against one another.

People had many a variety of these beaded curtains.

Some of the people in my neighborhood (next door, across the street, down the block, and blocks away neighbors) had the attractive wooden kind. Some had bright multicolored ones, and some had ones that were designed in diamond/oval shapes.

Door beads/beaded curtains are a creative way to add character and beauty into a place of residence or business.

The thought also brings to me a wonderful sense of nostalgia to what once was.

There are modern door beads and beaded curtains to decorate our homes with nowadays, but nothing will compare to the essence that held at a time when this style expressed the decade.

* * *

I remember when I was in the fourth grade. I had a teacher named Mrs. Yaffey. She was Jewish.

I attended an elementary school in Bayside, New York at the time— P.S. 203.

I wrote a play back then as an assignment in which I chose specific classmates to act out in roles I had created within my story. I even cast a student for the narration in between scenes that I had written.

This preparation took place among us all in our classroom.

I never received a low or bad grade on book reports so knew I could write well at an early age. Reading and writing were my best subjects.

After Mrs. Yaffey was impressed by one of my book reports— she to my surprise—gave me the lead role as Robinhood for our school play called "Potpourri".

I was not one who wanted to be in the spotlight, so I gave the part to a girl named Erica Goldstein. She had a narrator role in which I exchanged with her.

Throughout the days up until we were to perform on stage in front of an auditorium full of people we rehearsed and had to get our apparel and costumes ready.

I had to wear a white shirt, a black belt, and black tights as the narrator. "Robinhood" had to wear her cape and each other character according to their required specific wardrobe.

During opening night my mother later expressed to me that she was disappointed that I had such few lines in a small role. I don't think she liked that I gave up the lead part to someone else.

But things like that were not a big deal to me. I was not a child who liked being the center of attention.

My mother did not mean any harm, she was just a parent who was proud of her kid.

Fifteen

Lifestyle

I remember when the television stations would go off the air after midnight. There was no all-night, 24/7 broadcast to watch for most channels.

I remember when there was no 911 to call. We used to have to dial 0 to have the operator transfer us over to the police.

I remember when it cost sixty-five cents to ride public transportation. I remember when it was a two-dollar admittance into the movie theater to see a double feature.

I remember rotary and touch-tone phones.

I remember when we would stick metal hangers into broken television antennas to gain a clear reception on the old model tubes.

I remember so much of the good old days, too much to mention!

* * *

A lot has changed throughout the decades and throughout the years. Many good changes have brought convenience and enhancements into our lives.

There was a time when none of us were walking around with cell phones to text with or to reach the internet with and we had all got along fine in life for that time-span

Currently, I am sure none of us can imagine living without these items but back then way before these things were introduced to us, we maintained a period that corresponded to our habits and way of living during those eras.

Computers existed but they were not advanced as the ones we have now.

When we were out in public and needed to make a telephone call we had telephone booths on the street—some encased with glass doors for our privacy.

There were even telephone books inside the booths to aid us in making forward connections to locate people and places.

* * *

It's mandatory nowadays for many of us to have cellular/smart-phones and computers even when it pertains to our jobs.

Many of our employers and the various fields of work now fluently communicate with us and require the use of these apparatuses regarding our positions and assignments through the deployment of our androids, laptops, and/or computers.

Telecommunications has come very far and is so very essential to our lives in all aspects.

We have location features and GPS to let us know where we are, to help us to find a destination, and to sufficiently get us to our routes when our gadgets are performing accurately.

We can text message in private and for a quick connection, or to alert someone, or just for the mere advantage of convenience.

We can email and fax to ensure the prompt arrival of documents or to meet important deadlines, and so on.

We can build websites to conduct our own businesses or to advance within our own interpersonal or inherent skills, and to expand within our occupations from home if we choose to venture out more independently and dynamically.

There is so many resources in the operation and benefits which serve to a better lifestyle and way of living when it is utilized in a responsible and productive fashion.

Sixteen

Music

Music is one of the greatest things that we have on planet earth and in the heavens.

How could anyone imagine living in a world without music?

Aside from music highlighting festive events and activities, music hugely contributes to the health and wellness of our mind, body, and soul.

* * *

Oh, were the days back in the day when we blew the dust off the turntable needles.

When we rubbed alcohol on the track of vinyl record surfaces to remove or smooth out scratches that made the records skip.

How we would lay down or sit in relaxation tuned into the mellow songs or thumping beats, taking in lyrics of meaningful, artistic, and playful music.

Such a calm and effervescent moment in times.

* * *

Music relates our experiences as musical lyrics express thoughts, feelings, and scenarios identical to situations that some are not able to put into words.

Music can enhance or uplift one's mood when feeling happy or sad.

Music makes us want to dance.

Music is good for the soul no matter if one is young or they are old.

* * *

Dancing is a healthy and enjoyable exercise for anyone to enjoy or take part in if the moment hits them.

When the music plays to the tune of a favorite jam and that song makes you start to move to that enticing groove—do not resist.

Just dance and sing, do not be afraid to do your thing!

Seventeen

Happiness

I feel a great freedom that comes along with the balance and alignment with the universe.

The power to self-express and to reflect to us all the essential benefits that life has to offer.

Elements that are suitable and fulfilling to the needs of any aspiring individual, corresponding to the aids of a better health and state of well-being.

I find in not being at all afraid to acknowledge and to display what I truly know, feel, or believe effectively welcomes in a change and opens the doors to the reality that one naturally deserves.

One lives who they are by exuding their pure unrelenting

energy out into the cosmic field what a very courageous thing to step out onto the limb of chance reaching far away past to an area that is out of grasp, out of sight, then taking that jump into atmospheric range, a giant leap into faith.

An unwavering account of risk, dare to go to the edge. Dare to face the challenge of testing the waves, rowing in the tides, demanding the rewards of fate.

Going that extra mile minimizes the distance allowing the separated part of oneself to connect and to find infinite validation through compatibility.

The outer part of self can only recognize and return to the inner part once confirmation is identified, authenticated by truth.

If sections of one are hidden from their other missing pieces how or why should they find or even come back together as a whole?

Who wants to live in collision with one's own self? Not me. I would not.

The great and beautiful lesson that I have learned is the more that I take advantage of delighting in being real, in being myself, in putting myself above the restrictions of what is supposedly permitted by the world, I embrace the permission to not permit the world to limit to me and to my phenomenal outcomes.

* * *

Why spend precious moments wasting time on circumstances that do not bring about any true value or satisfaction within one's own purpose and desire?

Be who you are and live life without letting all of life hassles beguile and live you!

Fulfillment comes in all shapes, sizes, and mixtures, and if one is not exact and upfront about taking a portion of the opportunity that is within grab all of what is available will be put to drain.

Unwavering consistency is useless when it goes unaccounted for through not accepting one's own identity and design.

Other individual's unresolved issues are exactly what they are and not an associated factor in the determination of one's own beneficial succession.

Follow one's own heart and mind and not that of those who coerce or persuade in attempts to discourage.

* * *

I have noticed since my early youth that if there was something in life that I did not want then the circumstance was not going to work out for the best—or at all.

I cannot have anyone, or any situation persuaded, or forced upon me. I am too headstrong to be influenced by what others may try to impose on me.

When things in life I desired were granted to me or attained by my own accomplishing the circumstance always worked out favorably with long-lasting rewards.

I determine my happiness not what other people define what happiness is according to their standards or perception of what meets the requirements of a happy or content life condition.

Only I know the true source and components needed to define the attributes of my own fulfillment.

* * *

I find joy in having peace of mind. I find joy in the strength that God gave to me.

I found joy during bad times because when darkness was around me my light still shined, leading me straight to the path of my success.

True joy comes from the Lord.

The joy that I have the world did not give it to me, and the world cannot take it away—and that is the truth!

* * *

Happiness When It Comes To Animosity

I hate when people say let bygones be bygones.

Once I cut a person loose it is for keeps. Individuals have one time to mess up with me, they do not get a second chance.

If I dislike someone, if someone rubs me the wrong way, If I get a negative vibe about someone, or if someone does a wrongdoing towards me, that is it. There will never be a future within any type of association.

I have always been this way. I do not forgive, and I do not forget.

Forgiving someone has absolutely nothing to do with strength and not forgetting has absolutely nothing to do with not being able to move on when it comes to my point of view.

I do not know where some people get their mode of thinking from as I have heard people talk such reverse nonsense.

If someone helped one out a long, long time ago, and then they ended up needing a favor would it be wise to summarize that their generosity of being helpful was done a long time ago so I will just forget about it and not be considerate enough to return a good deed?

Hell, no.

So why should dirt done by others be forgotten about? One does not have to dwell on a situation and can go on with their life without making a truce.

If one was foolish enough to mend ties, depending on the circumstance, they'd just be going back to the exact situation as before, only worse.

Usually, it is the ones who caused the trouble to begin with who are eager to want bygones to be bygones.

I usually say bye and be gone.

It does not mean one is hurt by them—nobody cares about them, certain people who feel the way we have do not even think about these other people so obviously it is them who cannot move on.

I am an honest, straightforward person who does not put on airs, and who pulls no punches.

I am also an unconventional individual by nature.

Now, I know what scripture says and I am a living testimony to many accounts of how God has preserved and protected me throughout my life since childhood.

So, I mean no disregard.

However—and maybe I just have a different understanding of what forgiveness means— but with me, my definition of unforgiveness is if others did or tried to do dirt against me or wronged me in some way, I would not be compassionate or sympathetic toward them if something unfortunate happened in their life. I would feel that it was good for them, or they had gotten what they deserved.

I know God/Jesus asked us to love and forgive others yet that is a very hard thing for some of us to do as there are a lot of no good, devious, treacherous people out there in the world.

I do not apologize for the way I feel as I am entitled to my own manner of bearing.

I have thought this way since my teenage years and it has never spoiled or interfered in my happiness or contentment.

I am not suggesting to others that it is proper for them to hold or adopt this attitude, I just view things in a different light and can relate to other people who may share my same or similar standpoint or viewpoint.

To sum it all up what I am acknowledging is when I hear people say that forgiveness is for themselves it well may be for whatever it is they were holding onto inside.

But for me it is just about disliking trouble causing people, and not caring about them or their lives in the sense as if bad things were to occur or if I saw them in trouble, I would not go to help them. I do not see how feeling this way has any emotional grip or impact on my life whatsoever.

I do not in my adult life sit around to wish for bad things to happen to anyone I just live and appreciate the blessings that I have.

With me, God has allowed me to escape the many wrongdoings of others without them being able to have gotten the best of me.

It was the principle of the matter in the attempt and endeavors that had inspired the distaste in me along with not taking to their spirits harmoniously.

* * *

Despite how some of us may feel God prefers that we do things his way.

We, of course, do not have to associate with undesirable people—in fact we are not supposed to if they are not good or healthy to be around—and we do not even have to like them.

God takes care of people within his own time as people who continue in unwarranted or unjustified deeds reap what they sow.

God endows some of us with discernment and wisdom but for the most part he knows the insides and outsides of a person/people better than we do.

So, we leave all things up to God and he can speak to our hearts.

Eighteen

Goals

Those certain people who may have disliked, snubbed, laughed at you, or brushed you off. The particular job, school, or establishment that did not hire, admit, or accept you. Situations or circumstances in life that did not work out for you.

All occurrences many times play out as blessings in disguise.

Do not always take an unwelcoming or unfortunate turn of events as an insult, loss, or defeat.

In actuality, these incidents are favorable wins to success in better areas of life and with others that will prove to be advantageous.

There are one or two things I may have wanted when I was younger and did not get. I am so glad I do not have or desire these things now, as I am better off without them.

They were not bad, negative things, but things that were not in harmony with the balance within my alignment.

Other things may come at a time when we are ready for them, some things are not meant for us, and many things we just do not need.

We might have plenty of thoughts and ideas about how we would like to write our story. What we want to unfold as we turn the pages of our life.

However, God has a far more superior version of our story, and how it should be written. *God's direction in detail is a page-turner indeed!* A book about us that we are not able to put down. Authored with content by one who is brilliantly unmatched.

So let the Lord be the narrator in your life, because if you do, you are guaranteed to be a bestseller!

Nineteen

Relaxation

Just like success or personal fulfillment relaxation can mean different things to various people.

What one may find to relax another may find that same method to be annoying or agitating.

We are not to follow behind others for the sake of what is popular for the moment, we are to follow what is appropriate and best suited for our needs, desires, and wants that attribute to one's own fullness of well-being.

Twenty

Restfulness

Restfulness is more than sleep.

Many are not just tired physically by running around conducting everyday life. They are tired mentally or emotionally and seek to be set free from feeling bogged down in a crazy world.

Life experiences, life situations, life interactions can all contribute to overstep people's tolerance levels.

As one evolves while others stay or remain at the same levels of familiarity—certain types of people societal conditions, the media, and the government become a suffocating life nuisance.

Those who differ from what is frequently seen or encountered in usual occurrence get frustrated by unpleasant or undesirable common modes of attitude, behavior, and mentality that is considered ordinary for most.

Personal settings or predicaments can also cause mental and emotional exhaustion. What some need and/or require is a vacation from their regular boring routine or ongoing typicality of life.

Others need a permanent change of environment altogether.

Some people are not able to financially afford to place themselves in a more suitable atmosphere.

When mental, emotional, or even physical loads get to be enough or too much for one to handle they can just take it to the Lord.

He is always waiting, willing, and able to orchestrate a plan of restoration to aid one back into their pep.

True restfulness is found in letting go to rest in the arms of God.

www.ingramcontent.com/pod-product-compliance
Lightning Source LLC
Chambersburg PA
CBHW020644160726
47991CB00003B/1017